Y0-DWL-593

TOP 10 AMERICAN WOMEN'S OLYMPIC GOLD MEDALISTS

Christin Ditchfield

SPORTS TOP 10

Enslow Publishers, Inc.

40 Industrial Road   PO Box 38
Box 398   Aldershot
Berkeley Heights, NJ 07922   Hants GU12 6BP
USA   UK

http://www.enslow.com

Library of Congress Cataloging-in-Publication Data

Ditchfield, Christin.
    Top 10 American women's Olympic gold medalists / Christin Ditchfield.
        p. cm. — (Sports top 10)
    Includes bibliographical references and index.
    Summary: Profiles ten of the best American women's Olympic gold
medalists in history including Babe Didrikson, Peggy Fleming, Florence Griffith-
Joyner, and Kristi Yamaguchi.
    ISBN 0-7660-1277-8
    1. Athletes—United States—Biography—Juvenile literature. 2. Women
athletes—United States—Biography—Juvenile literature. 3. Women athletes—
Rating of—United States—Juvenile literature. 4. Olympics—History—Juvenile
literature. [1. Athletes. 2. Women athletes. 3. Olympics. 4. Women—Biography.]
I. Title: Top ten American women's Olympic gold medalists. II. Title. III. Series.
GV697.A1 D58 2000
796'.082'092273—dc21
    [B]   99-056060

Printed in the United States of America

10 9 8 7 6 5 4 3 2 1

To Our Readers: All Internet addresses in this book were active and appropriate
when we went to press. Any comments or suggestions can be sent by e-mail to
Comments@enslow.com or to the address on the back cover.

Illustration Credits: © 1995 Michelle Harvath, p. 42; © 1994 Michelle
Harvath, p. 45; © Robert Tringali, SportsChrome, Inc., pp. 7, 19; Courtesy of
Mary Lou Retton Entertainment, pp. 27, 29; Courtesy of UCLA Photography,
p. 22; Elite Management, p. 25; Nathan Bilow © 1998, pp. 35, 37;
SportsChrome, Inc., pp. 9, 21; Sports Information Office, Colorado State
University, pp. 39, 41; United States Olympic Committee Library, pp. 10, 13,
14, 17, 30, 33.

Cover Illustration: Nathan Bilow

Cover Description: Picabo Street

Interior Design: Richard Stalzer

CONTENTS

INTRODUCTION

DO WOMEN BELONG IN THE OLYMPIC GAMES? In 1896, the organizers of the first modern Olympics said "No." Most people in those days thought that women should not enter athletic competitions. They believed women's bodies were delicate and fragile. Too much physical activity could be dangerous to their health—and might even prevent them from being able to have children. Women just were not strong enough to endure the strain of competition. And after all, it was not "lady-like" to sweat!

At the Paris Games in 1900, women were allowed to participate in a few of the "less strenuous" sports, like golf and yachting. It was not until the 1920s that women could compete in a wider variety of events, including fencing, figure skating, and track and field. Even then, there were strict rules and regulations that limited what women could do.

In the one hundred years since women first competed in the Olympics, many things have changed. Thousands of women have now had the opportunity to represent their nations in the quest for Olympic glory. Their achievements have awed and inspired the world. Time and time again they have proved that they deserve their place in the Olympic Games.

The first woman to win an Olympic competition was an American, Margaret Abbott. She took the prize for first place in the ladies' golf tournament. Since then, many of the outstanding female Olympic athletes have come from the United States.

This book tells the stories of ten of these—perhaps the very best—who not only broke world records and won medals—but did it with style! Some showed that women could compete in the most physically demanding sports. Others had nerves of steel—they came through when the pressure was on. Three battled crippling childhood illness-es to achieve their success. And one athlete's performance even brought comfort to the nation after a terrible tragedy.

These courageous women refused to accept the limita-tions and boundaries that others had set for them. They did not give in to their own discouragement and disappoint-ments. They rose to meet their challenges; they pursued their dreams. Not everyone would agree that we have cho-sen the ten best women's olympians of all time—perhaps you can think of others. However, it is clear that the women in this book have earned the right to be called Olympic champions.

OLYMPIC STATISTICS

ATHLETE	YEAR	G	S	B	EVENTS
BONNIE BLAIR	1984, 1988,	5		1	Speed skating, 500-, 1,000-meter
	1992, 1994				
BABE DIDRIKSON	1932	2	1		Javelin; high jump;
					80-meter hurdles
PEGGY FLEMING	1968	1			Individual figure skating
FLORENCE GRIFFITH-JOYNER	1984, 1988	3	2		100-meter dash; 200-meter dash;
					4 x 100-, 4 x 400-meter relay
JACKIE JOYNER-KERSEE	1984, 1988,	3	1	2	Heptathlon; long jump
	1992, 1996				
MARY LOU RETTON	1984	1	2	2	Vault; Uneven Bars; Floor Ex.;
					All-Around; Team competition
WILMA RUDOLPH	1956, 1960	3		1	100-meter dash; 200-meter dash;
					4 x 100-meter relay
PICABO STREET	1994, 1998	1	1		Downhill; super-G
AMY VAN DYKEN	1996	4			50-meter freestyle;
					100-meter butterfly;
					4 x 100-meter freestyle relay;
					4 x 100-meter medley relay
KRISTI YAMAGUCHI	1992	1			Individual figure skating

G=GOLD   **S**=SILVER   **B**=BRONZE

Bonnie Blair

IT SEEMED LIKE BONNIE BLAIR WAS BORN to skate. All five of her older brothers and sisters raced in speed skating competitions. Bonnie's father refereed junior tournaments. By the time she was two years old, Bonnie was with the rest of the family on the ice. "I can't even remember learning how to skate," Blair later told a reporter. "It comes almost as naturally to me as walking."[1]

Bonnie Blair started competing at age four. As a teenager, she concentrated on Olympic-style speed skating, rather than the "pack" style that was popular at the local rink. It soon became obvious to the other skaters and coaches that Blair was something special. She had the talent that could take her all the way to the top. She had enthusiasm and determination—the heart of a true champion. The only thing she did not have was money. The Blair family could not afford the enormous expenses of coaching, equipment, and travel. Then the Champaign, Illinois, police department decided to step in.

Calling Blair "Champaign's Favorite Speeder," her hometown police force sold T-shirts and bumper stickers to help raise money for Blair's training.[2] They even held bake sales! The whole city rallied behind Blair and encouraged her to "go for the gold!"

And that's exactly what she did. From 1984 to 1994, Blair competed in four separate Olympic Games. She captured five gold medals and one bronze medal, making her the winningest American athlete in Winter Games history. *Sports Illustrated* named her "Sportswoman of the Year" in 1994. Her skating career had been phenomenal up to that

BONNIE BLAIR

Gliding along the ice, Bonnie Blair skates her way to Olympic gold.

time. She had broken records left and right, winning every competition there was to win. She had done it all. Or so everyone thought.

After her triumph at the Lillehammer Games, everyone expected the thirty-one-year-old skater to retire. But Blair had one more goal, one more dream. "To me, success means always striving for a personal best!" she explained.[3]

Blair wanted to be the first skater to race 500 meters in less than 39 seconds. Just a few months after the Olympics, she competed in the World Cup Championships. In spite of intense competition from younger and stronger skaters, Blair thrilled her family and fans with a record-breaking victory—taking the 500-meter race in just 38.69 seconds. With that race, she earned the title, "Fastest Speed Skater Ever."

Now Bonnie Blair could retire. She married fellow Olympic speed skater David Cruikshank and together they began raising their own family.

BONNIE BLAIR

BORN: March 18, 1964, Cornwall, New York.

RECORDS/MEDALS: Olympic gold-medal winner, 500-meter speed skating, 1988, 1992, 1994; Olympic gold-medal winner, 1,000-meter speed skating, 1992, 1994; Olympic bronze-medal winner, 1,000-meter speed skating, 1988.

HONORS: ABC's "Wide World of Sports" Athlete of the Year, 1992; United States Olympic Committee Sportswoman of the Year, 1992, 1994; Sullivan Award for the nation's best amateur athlete, 1992; Associated Press Female Athlete of the Year, 1994; *Sports Illustrated* Sportswoman of the Year, 1994; ESPY Award for Outstanding Female Athlete of the Year, 1995.

Her fist raised in triumph, Blair celebrates her Olympic victory at Lillehammer, Norway. A few months later, Blair set a world record at the 1994 World Championships.

Internet Address

http://www.olympic-usa.org/olympians/meet/bios/speedska/blair.html

BABE DIDRIKSON

Multi-sport star Babe Didrikson is considered by many to be the greatest woman athlete ever.

BABE DIDRIKSON

AT THE **1932 OLYMPIC GAMES** in Los Angeles, all eyes were on American track star Mildred "Babe" Didrikson. The crowds waited eagerly to see how she would fare against opponents from around the world. Didrikson was confident. She told reporters, "I'm out to beat everybody in sight, and that's just what I'm going to do!"[1]

She had good reason to expect success. An amazingly gifted athlete, Didrikson excelled in every sport she tried. And she tried quite a few. At one time or another, Didrikson competed in baseball, basketball, tennis, swimming, volleyball, and all of the various events included in the "track and field" category. As a young girl, she had hit so many home runs on the baseball field that her friends started calling her "Babe," after baseball superstar Babe Ruth.

A few months before the 1932 Summer Olympics, Didrikson had entered the National Track and Field Athletic Championships. At that time the rules allowed her to participate in as many events as she chose. In three hours, Didrikson competed in eight different events! She won the shot put, baseball throw, broad jump, javelin throw, and the 80-meter hurdles. She tied for first place in the high jump and placed fourth in the discus.

Now at the Olympics, the rules had changed. Didrikson could only compete in three events. She made her choices count. Didrikson won the gold medal in the javelin throw and the 80-meter hurdles. She tied for first in the high jump, but she was awarded the second-place silver medal when judges decided she had used a technique that did not meet Olympic regulations.

After the Olympic Games, in 1938, Didrikson married fellow Olympian, George Zaharias. In the meantime, Didrikson started taking golf lessons, with the idea of playing competitively in women's tournaments. With her trademark determination, Didrikson often practiced twelve hours a day. She bandaged her hands as they grew bloody and blistered. All of her hard work paid off. From the moment she began to compete, Babe Didrikson dominated women's golf. She won a total of 82 tournaments in her astonishing career.[2]

The only thing that could stop her was cancer. After numerous painful treatments, she was hospitalized for major surgery in 1953.

Babe was not about to give up. "All my life I've been competing—and competing to win," she said. "I came to realize that in its way, this cancer was the toughest opposition I'd faced yet. I made up my mind that I was going to lick it all the way!"[3]

Four months after surgery, Didrikson was back on the golf course. The next year, she won five major tournaments. But in 1956, Babe lost her battle with cancer. All over the world, people mourned the loss of the woman known as "The Greatest Female Athlete of the First Half of the Twentieth Century."

BABE DIDRIKSON

BORN: June 26, Port Arthur, Texas. Didrikson's birthyear is unknown. Historians believe she was born anywhere from 1911 to 1914.

DIED: September 27, 1956, Galveston, Texas.

RECORDS/MEDALS: Olympic gold-medal winner, javelin, 1932; Olympic gold-medal winner, 80-meter hurdles, 1932; Olympic silver-medal winner, high jump, 1932; Won 55 pro and amateur golf events, including 10 majors.

HONORS: Associated Press Female Athlete of the Year, 1932, 1945–47, 1950, 1954; chosen female "Athlete of the Half Century" by Associated Press, 1950; inducted into U.S. Track and Field Hall of Fame, 1974; inducted into the LPGA Hall of Fame, 1974; inducted into the International Women's Sports Hall of Fame, 1980; inducted into U.S. Olympic Hall of Fame, 1983.

After achieving Olympic success, Didrikson took up golf, and was soon a champion on the greens as well.

Internet Address
http://www.greatwomen.org/zhrias.htm

PEGGY FLEMING

Peggy Fleming entered the 1968 Winter Olympics as the reigning United States and World Champion women's figure skater. She left an Olympic champion.

IT WAS SO HORRIBLE THAT PEOPLE could hardly believe it—one of the worst tragedies in the history of American sports. On February 15, 1961, the entire United States Figure Skating team, eighteen skaters and sixteen coaches, died in a plane crash on the way to the World Championships in Prague, Czechoslovakia. An entire generation of American skaters was lost.

Eleven-year-old Olympic hopeful, Peggy Fleming, was devastated by the news. Her coach had been on the plane. In time, though, Fleming began working with a new coach. She knew that America's figure skating hopes and dreams rested largely on her shoulders. It was a lot of pressure for a young girl. Fleming was fifteen when she skated in her first Olympics in 1964. She performed well and placed sixth overall.

Over the next few years, Fleming continued to develop her artistic skills and technique. By the time the 1968 Olympics rolled around, Fleming had been crowned U.S. National Champion five years in a row. Twice she had won the World Championships. She skated with confidence, elegance, and grace. Her performance was superb. Explained a writer from *Sports Illustrated*, "Her skating appeared effortless, and therein lay its magic. She seemed to flow from one element to the next, seemingly weightlessly, like something blown about by the wind."[1]

This was the first time the Winter Olympics had been televised worldwide, live and in color. Millions of viewers tuned in to watch nineteen-year-old Peggy Fleming capture the gold medal. She captured their hearts as well.

As it turned out, Fleming was the only American, male or female, to win a gold medal in the 1968 Winter Games. Later that year, she went on to win her third World Championship. After retiring from amateur skating, Fleming began a long and successful professional skating career. She filmed commercials and television specials, and became a regular commentator for ABC Sports.

Peggy Fleming will always be remembered most for her gold medal performance in 1968. Her Olympic triumph comforted and encouraged a grieving nation and, at the same time, inspired a new generation of figure skaters. The impact of her victory is still felt today. Figure skating coach Linda Leaver explains, "Peggy's energy got the train of U.S. Figure Skating moving again. Once it got rolling, nothing has stopped it since."[2]

PEGGY FLEMING

BORN: July 27, 1948, San Jose, California.

RECORDS/MEDALS: Olympic gold-medal winner, women's figure skating, 1968; World champion, women's figure skating, 1966–1968.

HONORS: ABC's "Wide World of Sports" Athlete of the Year, 1967; Associated Press Female Athlete of the Year, 1968; Babe Didrikson Zaharias Award, 1968; inducted into the International Women's Sports Hall of Fame, 1981; inducted into U.S. Olympic Hall of Fame, 1983; Olympic Spirit Award, 1997.

Fleming, standing in the center, receives her gold medal at the 1968 Winter Olympic Games.

Internet Address

http://www.worldskatingmuseum.org/fleming.htm

FLORENCE GRIFFITH-JOYNER

DISAPPOINTED AND DISCOURAGED! That is how Florence Griffith felt after the 1984 Olympic Games in Los Angeles. The track star had been within a quarter of a second of winning the gold medal in the 200-meter race. But she had lost. She had to settle for second place and the silver medal. She did not take it well.

Griffith went home and got a job at a bank. At night she worked as a beautician, styling hair and nails. She spent her free time writing poetry and children's books. She continued to run, but not seriously. It seemed Florence Griffith had given up her athletic dreams.

But then in 1987, just one year away from the next Olympics, Griffith had a change of heart. She decided to start training again. Her new coach, Al Joyner, was an Olympic champion himself and the brother of Olympic superstar Jackie Joyner-Kersee. Al gave up his own career to help Florence make the most of hers. He put her through a challenging new workout. He added sit-ups, curls, and weight training to her routine.

By the time the 1988 track season began, Florence Griffith-Joyner was in the best shape of her life. She was also married to her coach. Griffith-Joyner drew attention everywhere she went, and not just with her athletic performance. With her long flowing hair and four-inch fingernails painted in elaborate designs, she looked more like a movie star than an athlete. She raced in wildly colored outfits that she designed herself. Fans affectionately nicknamed her "Flo-Jo."

Flo-Jo was flashy, but she was also fast. The 1988

Florence Griffith-Joyner waves the United States flag after victory at the 1988 Summer Olympics, held in Seoul, South Korea.

Olympic Games were hers. She captured the gold in the 100- and 200-meter dashes, and the 4 x 100-meter relay. She broke the world record in the 200 meters with a time of 21.34 seconds. It was official: Griffith-Joyner had now become "The Fastest Woman in the World." She rounded out her medal collection with another silver, this one for the 4 x 400-meter relay.

After retiring, Flo-Jo pursued her interests in acting, fashion design, and fitness. She and Al became parents of a little girl. Then in 1998, tragedy struck without warning. Florence Griffith-Joyner died suddenly at the age of thirty-eight. She had suffered a seizure in her sleep. Her death shocked and saddened everyone. President Bill Clinton announced, "America and the world has lost one of our greatest Olympians. We were dazzled by her speed, humbled by her talent, and captivated by her style."[1]

Bill Hybl, the president of the United States Olympic Committee, described Flo-Jo as a wonderful role model for girls and women everywhere. He added simply, "She will be missed."[2]

FLORENCE GRIFFITH-JOYNER

BORN: December 21, 1959, Los Angeles, California.

DIED: September 21, 1998, Mission Viejo, California.

COLLEGE: California State University-Northridge; UCLA.

RECORDS/MEDALS: Olympic gold-medal winner, 100-meter dash, 1988; Olympic gold-medal winner, 200-meter dash, 1988; Olympic gold-medal winner, 4 x 100-meter relay; Olympic silver-medal winner, 200-meter dash, 1984; Olympic silver-medal winner, 4 x 400-meter relay, 1988.

HONORS: Associated Press Female Athlete of the Year, 1988; UPI Female Athlete of the Year, 1988; Sullivan Award winner, 1988; USOC Sportswoman of the Year, 1988; Co-Chair of the President's Council on Physical Fitness and Sports, 1993; inducted into U.S. Track & Field Hall of Fame, 1995.

Few athletes have ever shown the flair and spirit of Florence Griffith-Joyner. Sadly, she died unexpectedly in 1998.

Internet Address

http://www.olympic-usa.org/olympians/meet/bios/joyner.html

JACKIE JOYNER-KERSEE

The "First Lady of Track and Field," Jackie Joyner-Kersee, competes in a long-jump competition while attending UCLA.

JACKIE JOYNER-KERSEE

WHEN A GIRL WAS BORN to the Joyner family in 1962, her grandmother insisted they name the baby after First Lady Jacqueline Kennedy. "Someday this girl will be the first lady of something!" she said.[1]

Grandmother was right. The little girl they called Jackie would grow up to be "The First Lady of Track and Field"— that is, the greatest multi-event track-and-field athlete of all time.

Jackie Joyner entered her first race when she was nine years old. At fourteen, she started practicing the long jump. As a high school student, Joyner won four straight national junior pentathlon championships. In college, though, she concentrated on her first love, basketball. Joyner's college coach saw her potential for greatness in track and field. He successfully convinced her to train for the Olympic heptathlon.

The heptathlon is a two-day competition in which athletes earn points for their performance in each of seven events. These events are the 200-meter dash, the high jump, the long jump, the javelin throw, the shot put, the 100-meter hurdles, and the 800-meter run. The victory goes to the athlete with the highest total score.

In 1984, Joyner competed at her first Olympic Games in Los Angeles, California. She came within .33 seconds of winning the gold medal in the heptathlon, and ended up with the silver instead. She had been so close! It was the last loss she would experience for a very long time.

After the Los Angeles Games, Joyner was determined to train even harder. She married her coach, Bob Kersee, and together they made a terrific team. Joyner-Kersee won the next nine heptathlons she entered. In 1986, she became the first woman to score more than 7,000 points in competition. Over and over, she set records and then broke them herself with even better performances.

At the 1988 Olympics, Joyner-Kersee took the gold medal in the heptathlon and the individual long jump. It turned out to be a great year for the whole family—Joyner-Kersee's sister-in-law, Florence Griffith-Joyner, also won gold medals in track-and-field competition. While Flo-Jo retired after the 1988 Games, Joyner-Kersee kept competing. She won the heptathlon gold again at the Barcelona Games in 1992, and took the bronze medal for the long jump.

Injuries and asthma sometimes made it difficult for her to compete, but Joyner-Kersee kept rising to the challenge. In 1996, at the age of thirty-four, she entered her fourth Olympic Games.

During the heptathlon competition, Joyner-Kersee suffered a hamstring injury and had to withdraw. It was a real disappointment. She had desperately wanted to earn a medal in what was sure to be her last Olympics. A few days after her withdrawal from the heptathlon, Joyner-Kersee somehow found the strength to compete in one last Olympic event—the long jump. When she won the bronze medal, she was thrilled. In four appearances at the Olympics, Jackie Joyner-Kersee never went home empty-handed.

JACKIE JOYNER-KERSEE

BORN: March 3, 1962, East St. Louis, Missouri.

COLLEGE: UCLA.

RECORDS/MEDALS: Olympic gold-medal winner, heptathlon, 1988, 1992; Olympic gold-medal winner, long jump, 1988; Olympic silver-medal winner, heptathlon, 1984; Olympic bronze-medal winner, long jump, 1992, 1996; World champion, heptathlon, 1987, 1991; World champion, long jump, 1987, 1993.

HONORS: Honda Broderick Cup for collegiate woman athlete of the year, 1985; Sullivan Award, 1986; *Track and Field News* Athlete of the Year, 1986; USOC Sportswoman of the Year, 1986–1987; Associated Press Female Athlete of the Year, 1987; *Sporting News* Sportsman of the Year (only woman to win), 1988; Flo Hyman Award, 1988.

In 1986, Joyner-Kersee became the first woman to score over 7,000 points in a heptathlon competition.

Internet Address

http://www.olympic-usa.org/olympians/meet/bios/kersee.html

MARY LOU RETTON

IT WAS ONE OF THE GREATEST MOMENTS in Olympic history. It was a moment Mary Lou Retton had worked toward for nine years. Half the world watched on television as the sixteen-year-old gymnast hurtled down the runway to the vaulting horse. Hitting the springboard, she flipped through the air and nailed a perfect landing. The nine thousand spectators at the Pauley Pavilion leapt to their feet, screaming wildly. In homes around the globe, people smiled, cheered, and cried tears of joy for the teenager from West Virginia.

Retton had just vaulted her way to Olympic superstardom. She scored a perfect 10 in what *Sports Illustrated* would later call "The Vault Without Fault."[1] That vault put Retton in first place in the individual all-around competition. She became the first American woman to capture a gold medal in any gymnastics event. Later in the week, she won two silver medals in the team all-around and the individual vault. She earned bronze medals in the uneven bars and the floor exercise. Retton's total of five medals topped that of any other athlete in the 1984 Summer Olympic Games. Her powerful and dynamic style had changed the sport of gymnastics forever.

Overnight, Retton became an international celebrity. Her face appeared on the covers of *Life, Seventeen, Newsweek, Sports Illustrated,* and *Time* magazines. Everyone loved her. She was bubbly and friendly and down-to-earth, full of confidence and charm. The media described her as the ultimate "girl-next-door." She reminded everyone of their daughter or sister or niece.

Mary Lou Retton took her home nation by storm with her perfect performance at the 1984 Summer Olympics in Los Angeles, California.

With her trademark smile and gold medal performance in 1984, Retton inspired an entire generation of young girls to participate in gymnastics. Twelve years later, for the first time ever, the American women's gymnastics team captured the team gold. Three of the seven members of the 1996 team said they had decided to become gymnasts while watching Retton on TV.[2]

To this day, Mary Lou Retton remains one of the most popular and widely recognized athletes in the world. She travels and speaks to groups of people all over the country, encouraging them to pursue their dreams. Retton is thrilled to hear that more and more young people are getting involved in sports. "Participating in a sport teaches you so much!" she exclaims. "It teaches you about sacrifice and discipline, about teamwork, about setting a goal and working to achieve it, determination, dedication. . . . All of those things that I learned in my athletic career I now carry into my everyday life as a wife, as a mother—in everything I do!"[3]

MARY LOU RETTON

BORN: January 24, 1968, Fairmont, West Virginia.

COLLEGE: University of Texas.

RECORDS/MEDALS: Olympic gold-medal winner, gymnastics all-around, 1984; Olympic silver-medal winner, vault, 1984; Olympic silver-medal winner, team, 1984; Olympic bronze-medal winner, uneven bars, 1984; Olympic bronze-medal winner, floor exercise, 1984.

HONORS: *Sports Illustrated* Woman of the Year, 1984; Associated Press Female Athlete of the Year, 1984; inducted into U.S. Olympic Hall of Fame, 1985; Special Advisor to the President's Council on Physical Fitness, 1993; inducted into International Women's Sports Hall of Fame, 1993; Flo Hyman Award, 1995; Official White House Delegate, Winter Olympics, 1998.

Retton's success has made her popular around the world. Among her honors was becoming the first woman to be chosen to appear on the cover of the Wheaties cereal box.

Internet Address

http://www.olympic-usa.org/games/ga_2_5_71.html

WILMA RUDOLPH

Wilma Rudolph overcame numerous childhood illnesses to become a world-class athlete.

WILMA RUDOLPH

MIRACULOUS! THIS IS THE ONLY WAY to describe the Wilma Rudolph story. Rudolph was born in Tennessee in 1940, the seventeenth of nineteen children. Premature at birth, she weighed only four and a half pounds. At four years old, Rudolph could not even walk, let alone run. She had contracted polio, a disease that crippled her and damaged her immune system. When she caught pneumonia and scarlet fever, doctors were sure she would die.

But somehow, the little girl survived. Wilma's mother massaged her deformed legs every day and took her to physical therapy twice a week. With the help of her brothers and sisters, six-year-old Wilma learned to hop around on one foot. By the time she was eight years old, she could walk with special leg braces. By age ten, she only needed special shoes. When Rudolph turned eleven, she started to run, and from then on, nothing held her back.

Wilma Rudolph played basketball in high school, but her coach recognized her talent for track and encouraged her to develop it. He gave her good advice. Rudolph turned out to be a racing sensation. In four years of high school track, she won every single race she entered.

At the 1956 Olympic Games in Australia, sixteen-year-old Rudolph was part of the American team that won the bronze medal in the 4 x 100-meter relay. Four years later, in time for the 1960 Olympics, Rudolph hit her peak. The media compared her to a gazelle—graceful and elegant. *Time* magazine observed, "From the moment she first sped down the track in Rome's Olympic Stadium, there was no doubt that she was the fastest woman the world had ever seen."[1]

Rudolph captured the gold medal in the 100-meter dash, tying the world record in the process. She set a new record in the 200-meter dash for her second gold medal. She then helped her team come from behind to win the 4 x 100-meter relay, her third gold medal. The little girl who could not walk had come a long way!

Rudolph told people, "The triumph can't be had without the struggle. And I know what struggle is."[2] With amazing courage, she had overcome incredible odds to excel in sports and in life. Later, Rudolph set up her own organization, the Wilma Rudolph Foundation, to help underprivileged children develop their own athletic gifts and pursue their dreams.

WILMA RUDOLPH

BORN: June 23, 1940, Clarksville, Tennessee.

DIED: November 12, 1994, Brentwood, Tennessee.

COLLEGE: Tennessee State University.

RECORDS/MEDALS: Olympic gold-medal winner, 100-meter dash,
1960; Olympic gold-medal winner, 200-meter dash, 1960;
Olympic gold-medal winner, 4 x 100-meter relay, 1960;
Olympic bronze-medal winner, 4 x 100-meter relay, 1956.

HONORS: Sullivan Award winner, 1961; Associated Press Female
Athlete of the Year, 1960–1961; inducted into U.S. Track &
Field Hall of Fame, 1974; inducted into International Women's
Sports Hall of Fame, 1980; inducted into U.S. Olympic Hall of
Fame, 1983.

Wilma Rudolph (left) poses for a picture with the members of the
1960 Olympic champion United States 4 x 100-meter women's
relay team.

Internet Address
http://greatwomen.org/rudlph.htm

Picabo Street

FOR THE FIRST SIX YEARS OF HER LIFE, America's future skiing sensation did not have a first name. She was simply known as "Baby Girl" Street. Her parents had an unusual lifestyle. They liked being different. But when the Street family decided to go on a vacation trip to Mexico, they realized that their "Baby Girl" needed a legal name for her passport. They chose the name Picabo (pronounced peek-a-boo), an American Indian word that means "shining waters."

Street loved sports. She played basketball, football, and soccer with all the boys in her neighborhood. "Not only did I want to be as good as the boys, I wanted to be better," she told a reporter.[1]

Picabo Street also enjoyed skiing. By the time she was in high school, it was obvious that she had a special talent for the slopes. At sixteen, she held the title "Western Junior Champion." At seventeen, she won the national junior downhill event and the super-G event (super giant slalom). The U.S. Olympic Team invited Street to join them. It was a tremendous honor.

At first, things did not go very well for Street. She had the talent to make the team, but not the work ethic. Her wild, fun-loving personality got in the way of her training. She lacked focus and discipline. Coach Paul Major explained, "Picabo burst onto the ski team with natural talent. She threw herself down the hill. No obstacles. But she relied on natural talent to keep her on the team. She didn't know the stakes had been raised."[2]

When Street showed up at training camp, she was out

PICABO STREET

Picabo Street celebrates on the medal stand after winning the super-G event at the 1998 Olympics. The super-G is also known as the super-giant slalom.

of shape and full of attitude. The coaches quickly kicked her off the team. The embarrassment turned out to be the wake-up call she needed. She decided to dedicate herself wholeheartedly to her skiing. She put in all the work it would take to become a champion. Her performance picked up and her attitude improved. She was soon invited to rejoin the U.S. team.

"As my results got better, I got hungrier," she said. "I just started chomping at the bit a little more."[3]

Street proved she could compete with the "best of the best" when she won the silver medal in the women's downhill at the 1994 Winter Games. Her hard work and dedication had produced the results she was looking for. And she would continue to improve. At the 1998 Games in Nagano, Japan, Picabo Street captured her first gold medal in the super-G.

PICABO STREET

BORN: April 3, 1971, Triumph, Idaho.

RECORDS/MEDALS: Olympic gold-medal winner, super-G, 1998; Olympic silver-medal winner, downhill, 1994; World Championships, silver medalist (combined), 1993; World Cup downhill series title, 1995, first by a U.S. woman.

HONORS: USOC Sportswoman of the Year, 1995.

Street missed most of the 1996–1997 ski season because of a knee injury. That made her victory in 1998 all the more remarkable.

Internet Address

http://www.usskiteam.com/alpine/bios/street00.htm

WHEN AMY VAN DYKEN WAS TEN MONTHS OLD, her doctor had bad news for her parents. "She has the worst case of asthma I've ever seen."[1] Throughout her childhood, breathing problems plagued Amy. Her allergies and asthma kept her from enjoying normal everyday activities.

"Kids used to laugh at me," Van Dyken later recalled. "They'd have their little necklaces hanging around their necks. I'd have my inhaler. I couldn't go on field trips. I couldn't play basketball. I couldn't even play tag. I had a hard time laughing at a joke."[2]

Something as simple as climbing a flight of stairs left Van Dyken exhausted and out of breath. When she turned six, another doctor suggested that she take swimming lessons. He thought it might help strengthen her lungs. Van Dyken did not become a swimming sensation overnight. In fact, it was six years before she could swim from one end of the pool to the other without collapsing and gasping for air.

It may have been difficult at first, but Amy Van Dyken loved swimming. As she got older, she showed her coaches that she had a talent for the sport. In high school, Van Dyken made the swim team and won the state championships in the 50-meter freestyle and the 100-yard butterfly events. She was named Colorado Swimmer of the Year twice. Her success continued in college, where she became the NCAA champion and began setting world records. Still, Van Dyken battled asthma. There were times when she collapsed or fainted during practices and competitions. Some people suggested that she take stronger medications for her health. But many of the stronger medications had

When she was young, Amy Van Dyken had such a bad case of asthma that she found it hard to perform everyday activities. She took up swimming because a doctor felt it might help strengthen her lungs.

ingredients that were banned by the Olympic Committee, and Van Dyken was determined to become an Olympic champion. So she struggled on, with less-effective medicines.

Amy Van Dyken did not quite qualify for the 1992 Olympics. Just four years later, she was one of the fastest swimmers in the world. Everyone expected her to do well at the 1996 Atlanta Olympics, but Van Dyken surpassed even the highest expectations with her incredible performance. She won the 50-meter freestyle, the 100-meter butterfly, the 4 x 100-meter medley relay, and the 4 x 100-meter freestyle relay. Amy Van Dyken became the first woman in history to win four gold medals in a single Olympics.

"For all the kids out there struggling," she said, "If you can keep plugging away, something will come of it!"[3]

AMY VAN DYKEN

BORN: February 15, 1973, Englewood, Colorado.

COLLEGE: Colorado State University.

RECORDS/MEDALS: Olympic gold-medal winner, 50-meter freestyle, 1996; Olympic gold-medal winner, 100-meter butterfly, 1996; Olympic gold-medal winner, 4 x 100-meter freestyle relay, 1996; Olympic gold-medal winner, 4 x 100-meter medley.

HONORS: NCAA Swimmer of the Year, 1994; Associated Press Female Athlete of the Year, 1996; ARETE Courage in Sports Award, 1996; USOC Sportswoman of the Year, 1996. ESPY Award for Outstanding Female Athlete of the Year, 1997.

At the 1996 Summer Games in Atlanta, Georgia, Van Dyken became the first woman to win four gold medals in a single Olympics.

Internet Address

http://www.usswim.org/olympics/vandyken.htm

KRISTI YAMAGUCHI

From the time she was four years old, Kristi Yamaguchi knew she wanted to be an Olympic figure skater. She would spend hours at the rink each day.

KRISTI YAMAGUCHI

WHEN PEOPLE DESCRIBE KRISTI YAMAGUCHI, they usually choose words like "graceful," "elegant," "beautiful," and "expressive." America's gold-medal-winning figure skater is certainly all of those things. She is also tough, courageous, and determined. It may have seemed as though she glided through the Olympics effortlessly. In reality, Yamaguchi had worked very hard to achieve her success.

The odds were against her from the beginning. Yamaguchi was born with deformed feet that turned unnaturally inward. Doctors put her in plaster casts with metal rods to try to straighten her crooked feet. The casts had to be changed twice a month until she was two years old. She had a hard time learning to walk. Kristi's mother, Carole, encouraged her daughter to try dancing, ballet, ice skating— any activities that might help her develop strength in her legs. Kristi Yamaguchi loved the ice skating. As a four-year-old, she watched skater Dorothy Hamill on television. Yamaguchi knew then that she wanted to be an Olympic figure skater.

"When I look back on it, I worked incredibly hard for a little kid," Yamaguchi said later. "I would not get off the ice until I did some particular move right or until I did something a certain number of times. From the time I was six, I kept bugging my mom, 'Let's go skating, let's go skating.' I had my Dorothy Hamill doll, and I took it with me everywhere."[1]

Kristi Yamaguchi spent hours at the rink, starting at 5:00 A.M. each day. She gave most of her free time to skating-related activities or to homework and make-up work from the school classes she missed during competitions. She did not have time to play. Yamaguchi began competing in both singles and pairs competitions as a junior skater. With her partner, Rudy Galindo, she won several junior championship titles. They also did well in senior competition. In 1989, Galindo and Yamaguchi won the National Pairs title.

Yamaguchi was not as pleased with her singles results. She consistently came in second in the national competitions. The title was always just out of reach. After giving it a lot of thought, Yamaguchi decided to stop skating in pairs events. She devoted all of her training and practice time to improving her singles skating.

It turned out to be the right decision for her. She won the World Championships in 1991 and 1992. She then captured the 1992 U.S. National Championships, earning the title that had eluded her for so long. To cap it all off, 1992 brought her the gold medal at the Olympics in Albertville, France. By being dedicated and determined, Kristi Yamaguchi had made her childhood dream come true!

KRISTI YAMAGUCHI

BORN: July 12, 1971, Hayward, California.

RECORDS/MEDALS: Olympic gold-medal winner, individual women's figure skating, 1992; World champion, individual women's figure skating, 1991–1992; U.S. National champion, figure skating, 1992; U.S. National Champion, pairs figure skating, 1989.

After winning a National Pairs title, Yamaguchi decided to focus on the singles competition. Her hard work paid off when she won the gold medal at the 1992 Winter Olympics.

Internet Address

http://www.olympic-usa.org/olympians/meet/bios/figureskating/yamagu.html

CHAPTER NOTES

Bonnie Blair

1. Anne Janette Johnson, *Great Women in Sports* (Detroit: Visible Ink Press, 1996), p. 41.

2. Joe Layden, *Women in Sports* (Los Angeles: General Publishing Group, 1997), p. 30.

3. "The Legacy," *U.S.O.C. Online*, n.d., <http:www.olympic-usa.org> (January 15, 1999).

Babe Didrikson

1. Robert Markel, Susan Waggoner, and Marcella Smith, *The Women's Sports Encyclopedia* (New York: Henry Holt and Company, Inc., 1997), p. 203.

2. Jane Leder, *Grace and Glory: A Century of Women in the Olympics* (Chicago: Multi-Media Partners Ltd., 1996), p. 34.

3. Russell Freedman, *Teenagers Who Made History* (New York: Holiday House, Inc., 1961).

Peggy Fleming

1. Anne Janette Johnson, *Great Women in Sports* (Detroit: Visible Ink Press, 1996), p. 170.

2. Biography/Fact Sheet, "Peggy Fleming," Courtesy of International Management Group, New York, NY, 1998.

Florence Griffith-Joyner

1. Dick Patrick, "Track Star Blazed Trail," *USA Today*, September 22, 1998, p. C-1.

2. Ibid.

Jackie Joyner-Kersee

1. Jane Leder, *Grace and Glory: A Century of Women in the Olympics* (Chicago: Multi-Media Partners Ltd., 1996), p. 74.

Mary Lou Retton

1. Mary Lou Retton and Bela Karolyi, *Mary Lou Retton: Creating an Olympic Champion* (New York: McGraw-Hill Book Company, 1986), p. 158.

2. Nancy H. Kleinbaum, *The Magnificent Seven* (New York: Bantam Books, 1996), pp. 4, 17, 88.

3. Personal interview with Mary Lou Retton, February 24, 1999.

Wilma Rudolph

1. Jane Leder, *Grace and Glory: A Century of Women in the Olympics* (Chicago: Multi-Media Partners Ltd., 1996), p. 56.

2. Anne Janette Johnson, *Great Women in Sports* (Detroit: Visible Ink Press, 1996), p. 405.

Picabo Street
1. Anne Janette Johnson, *Great Women in Sports* (Detroit: Visible Ink Press, 1996), p. 451.

2. Ibid., p. 453.

3. Joe Layden, *Women in Sports* (Los Angeles: General Publishing Group, 1997), p. 230.

Amy Van Dyken
1. Anne Janette Johnson, *Great Women in Sports* (Detroit: Visible Ink Press, 1996), p. 484.

2. Ibid.

3. Rick Warner, "Van Dyken Wins Record 4th Gold," *Washingtonpost.com*, July 27, 1996, <http//www.washingtonpost.com> (January 15, 1999).

Kristi Yamaguchi
1. Anne Janette Johnson, *Great Women in Sports* (Detroit: Visible Ink Press, 1996), p. 534.

INDEX